In the Solitude of Cotton Fields

GW00862518

Published by Methuen 2001

This edition published in 2001 by
Methuen Publishing Ltd
215 Vauxhall Bridge Road
London SW1V 1EJ

www.methuen.co.uk

Dans la Solitude des Champs de Coton
copyright © 1986 Éditions de Minuit
Translation copyright © 2001 by Jeffrey Wainwright
Introduction copyright © 2001 by Maria Delgado
The authors and translators have asserted their moral rights.

Methuen Publishing Ltd reg. number 3543167

ISBN 0 413 77177 6

A CIP catalogue record for this book is available at the British Library

Typeset by SX Composing DTP, Rayleigh, Essex
Transferred to digital printing 2004

atc presents

IN THE SOLITUDE OF COTTON FIELDS

by bernard-marie koltès
new translation by jeffrey wainwright

first performed at the aldwych tube station, london
21 september 2001

IN THE SOLITUDE OF COTTON FIELDS

by bernard-marie koltès
translation jeffrey wainwright

CAST

the dealer **david whitehead**
the client **zubin varla**

director **gordon anderson**
designer **thomas hadley**
lighting designer **zerlina hughes**

production manager **dan watkins**
company stage manager **tracy mcilroy**

press agent **anne mayer 020 7254 7391**
marketing **mark slaughter 020 8858 2783**
graphic design **mark goddard 020 7221 5028**

executive producer **emma dunton**
administrator **judith kilvington**

With special thanks to Barry Wilkinson at London Underground and to Hetty Shand

BIOGRAPHIES

gordon anderson director

Gordon is the new Artistic Director of ATC and his directorial credits include productions for some of the UK's leading theatre and opera companies, such as the English Touring Opera, Broomhill Opera, Manchester Royal Exchange, Royal Court Theatre, The Lyric Theatre Hammersmith and the Gate Theatre.

david westhead the dealer

After leaving RADA David began his career with ATC in the acclaimed production of *Faustus*. Since then he has played many leading roles at the Royal Shakespeare Company, Royal National Theatre and Royal Court including *Travesties, Tamburlaine, A Jovial Crew, Mojo* and *Talk of the City*, as well as the title roles in *The Changeling, The Man of Mode, The Prince's Play* and *The Libertine*. Film and TV roles include Arthur Thwaite in *The Lakes*, DCI Peter Murray in *My Fragile Heart*, Nick Costello in *Grafters*, Ned Carson in *Wilde*, George Mackie in the BAFTA-nominated *Donovan Quick* and Bertie, Prince of Wales, in the Oscar-nominated *Mrs Brown*. He will be seen later this year in *Safe House* for the BBC and alongside Stockard Channing and Jonathan Pryce in the film *Confessions of an Ugly Stepsister*.

zubin varla the client

Zubin trained at the Guildhall School of Music and Drama. He has just completed a successful season playing Caliban in *The Tempest*, directed by James Macdonald for the Royal Shakespeare Company. His work at the RSC includes *Bartholemew Fair, Faust, Romeo and Juliet,* and the title role in Koltès' *Roberto Zucco*. Other theatre credits include *A Day Like Today* for the Push Festival/Young Vic, *Antigone* for Warehouse Productions, *Beautiful Thing* at Duke of York's and the role of Judas in *Jesus Christ Superstar* at the Lyceum. His film and TV credits include *Dalziel and Pascoe, Crocodile Shoes* and the film *Jacob* directed by Sir Peter Hall.

thomas hadley designer

Thomas's design credits include *The Threesome*, Lyric Theatre Hammersmith, *The Silverlake*, Wilton's Music Hall and *Who's Afraid of Virginia Woolf*, Nottingham Playhouse. Thomas has also worked extensively in video and installation. Forthcoming work includes the video for the world tour of Faithless, video projections for the ENO productions and 'AI' for Amnesty International.

zerlina hughes lighting designer

Zerlina graduated from Goldsmiths College in 1991. Since then she has
worked in the opera, architectural lighting, television and film - in which
medium she was assistant director Mike Leigh on three films *Naked,
Secret & Lies* and *Career Girls*. In addition to Zerlina's previous work for
ATC she has extensive stage lighting credits on productions for some of
the UK's leading theatre and opera companies including the RNT,
Nottingham Playhouse, Glasgow Citizens Theatre, Scottish Opera Go
Round and Scottish Opera.

dan watkins production manager

Dan has worked extensively over the last ten years in theatre and opera,
from the west end to both national and international touring. Dan is
managing director for VGroup Creative Management, which provides
production and event management services to the entertainment industry.
Dan also works as a technical theatre consultant; recent projects include
Jersey Opera House, Keswick Theatre and Westminster School Theatre.

tracy mcilroy company stage manager

Tracy's theatre credits include The Wrestling School, Lyric Theatre
Hammersmith, Birmingham Stage Company, London Bubble.
She also runs her own design company called More Versatile.

emma dunton executive producer

Emma recently joined ATC. Previously she has worked at Volcano
Theatre Company, the British Council and on low-budget feature
films in Los Angeles.

judith kilvington administrator

Judith previously worked at Imperial College on a grant funded by the
Europe Against AIDS programme and at Goldsmiths College in the
Centre for Cultural Studies.

company information

Established in 1980 ATC has toured through the UK and internationally with celebrated productions such as *Faust* and *Handbag* and has recently collaborated with a wide range of creative talent including Laurie Anderson, Mark Ravenhill and Rose English.

This year ATC enters an exciting new phase in its life with the appointment of the acclaimed director Gordon Anderson as Artistic Director.

"A key area of development will be our commitment to giving British audiences the opportunity to experience the very best of contemporary international work."

The company will be developing and commissioning innovative new work which will be a razor-sharp interrogation of contemporary values. ATC's emphasis is on challenging the boundaries of the existing forms of live theatre and on instigating eclectic and surprising artistic collaborations.

"The play should not be about something but rather be the something itself." PETER HANDKE

The collaboration between translator Jeffrey Wainwright and director Gordon Anderson that this production represents, attempts to maintain the uncompromising edge and peculiarity of Koltès' language. In eschewing the traditional venue of an established performance space for 'alternative' locations like Aldwych tube station, the production continues a trend of stagings of Koltès in appropriated non-theatre spaces, further reinforcing the concerns around space and place which infuse the dramatist's writing.

MARIA M. DELGADO Queen Mary, University of London August 2001

In the Solitude of Cotton Fields

Bernard-Marie Koltès

Methuen Drama

Bernard-Marie Koltès:

Chronology

1948 Birth of Bernard-Marie Koltès (9 April) at Metz, a town in the Eastern part of France. His father, a professional soldier, was away in Algeria for much of the 1950s.

1958–62 Koltès's secondary schooling began against a background of bombings and disturbances as the crisis of the Algerian conflict pushed France to the brink of civil war.

1967 After completing school in Metz, Koltès went to Strasbourg, where he attended courses at the School of Journalism. He also studied music, and even considered becoming a professional organist.

1968 In January he saw Maria Casarès, at Strasbourg, playing the central role in Seneca's *Medea*; this was his first visit to a theatre and had an profound effect on him. During the May 1968 occupations of colleges and factories Koltès avoided political involvement. In the Summer he travelled to Paris, and then to New York.

1969 First attempt at writing for the theatre: a stage adaptation of Gorki's *My Childhood*, entitled *Les Aertumes [Bitternesses]*; he sent the play to Hubert Gignoux, director of the Strasbourg National Drama School, asking for advice.

1970 Koltès directed a few friends in a production of his play at the Théâtre du Quai, Strasbourg (performances in May and June). Hubert Gignoux saw the production and invited Koltès to join his course in the *régie* (technical) section of the School. He joined, but dropped out during his second year.

1971 He wrote and directed his second and third plays in the same little student Théâtre du Quai: *La Marche [The March]*, based on the Song of Songs, and *Procès Ivre [Drunken Trial]*, based on Dostoyevski's *Crime and Punishment*.

1972 *L'Héritage [The Inheritance]* broadcast on local Radio-

Alsace and then again on France Culture (produced by Lucien Attoun) with Maria Casarès.

1973 *Récits Morts [Dead Stories]* directed by Koltès at the Théâtre du Quai. During the 1970s Koltès earned little or nothing from his writing and took casual jobs (e.g. selling tickets in Strasbourg cinemas).

1974 A second play broadcast, first on Radio Alsace and afterwards on France Culture: *Des Voix Sourdes [Deaf/Muffled Voices]*.

1975–6 Koltès moved to Paris and wrote his first novel, *La Fuite à Cheval très loin dans la ville [The Flight on Horseback far into the Town]* (dated September 1976). The typescript circulated among friends for some years before being published by Éditions de Minuit in 1984.

1977 Wrote a dramatic monologue *La Nuit juste avant les forêts [The Night just before the Forests]* for actor Yves Ferry (whom he had known at the Strasbourg Drama School) and directed him in a performance given on the fringe of the Avignon Theatre Festival. Invited by Bruno Boeglin to observe a series of actors' workshops based on the stories of J. D. Salinger and to write a play inspired by them, he wrote *Sallinger* [sic],directed by Boeglin and performed during the 1977/8 season at his El Dorado theatre in Lyon.

1978 Journey to West Africa, where he visited friends working on a construction site in Nigeria.

1979 Returned to West Africa, visiting Mali and Ivory Coast; six month trip to Nicaragua (just before the Sandanista revolution) and to Guatemala, during which he wrote *Combat de nègre et de chiens [Black Battles with Dogs]*. The play was published as a 'tapuscrit' by Théâtre Ouvert – i.e. a limited number of typescripts which are made for circulation among theatre professional so as to encourage the dissemination of new theatre writing.

1980 Radio broadcast on France Culture of *Combat de nègre et de chiens*. The text received its first commercial publication in the 'Théâtre Ouvert'; series of Stock (Paris) together with *La Nuit juste avant les forêts*.

1981 Four month visit to New York. Koltès beginning to be known in theatre circles: *La Nuit just avant les forêts* revived at the Petit Odéon with the actor Richard Fontana. Received a commission for a play by the Comédie Française. Plans made with Françoise Kourilsky for a production of *Combat de nègre et de chiens* in New York.

1982 Returned to New York for world première of *Combat de négre et de chiens* at Theatre La Mama: the English translation, by Matthew Ward, was originally entitled *Come Dog, Come Night*. At Koltès's insistence, it was later changed to *Struggle of the Dogs and the Black* and published under this title, first in the collection of the New York Ubu Repertory Theatre (1982) and later by Methuen in *New French Plays* (1989). Koltès translated Athol Fugard's *The Blood Knot* for production at the Avignon Festival.

1983 Patrice Chéreau opened his new Théâtre des Amandiers at Nanterre (on the outskirts of Paris) with the French première of *Combat de nègre et de chiens*. The set (by Richard Peduzzi) was monumental and the cast star-studded: Michel Piccoli, Philippe Léotard, Miriam Boyer, Sidiki Bakaba; the critics were mostly enthusiastic: until his death at the end of the decade, Koltès was widely accepted as the most important new voice in French theatre.

From this point on he was able to live from his writing, though he earned more from foreign (especially German) productions than from the exploitation of his work in France. Worked briefly as 'dramaturge' with François Regnault on Chéreau's production of *Les Paravents [The Screens]* by Jean Genet; together they published *La Famille des Orties [The Nettle Family]*.

1984 Journey to Senegal. Publication of La Nuit juste avant les forêts (see 1977). Four different productions of *Combat de nègre et de chiens* in German theatres (Frankfurt, Tübingen, Wuppertal and Munich).

1985 Publication of *Quai ouest* by Éditions de Minuit; world première of the play given in Dutch at the Publiekstheater, Amsterdam.

1986 French première of *Quai ouest*, directed by Patrice Chéreau, with Maria Casarès in the cast, at the Théâtre des Amandiers. The critics were again impressed by the writing, but blamed Chéreau and Peduzzi for crushing the play beneath a monumental production. Koltès responded to a commission by the Avignon Festival for a play in a series with the title 'Osier aimer' ['To dare to love'] with a short play, *Tabataba*, about someone who 'dares to love' his motorcycle. Publication of *Dans le solitude des champs de coton [In the Solitude of the Cotton Fields]* by Minuit.

1987 First production of *Dans la solitude des champs de coton* by Patrice Chéreau at Nanterre. the role of the Client was taken by Laurent Malet and that of The Dealer by Isaach de Bankolé. In subsequent seasons Chéreau revived this production, taking the role of The Dealer himself; this provoked a temporary break with Koltès, who insisted that he had written the role of The Dealer for a black actor.

1988 Two major firsts for Koltès: *Le Retour au désert [Return to the Desert]* received its première in a production by Patrice Chéreau at the Théâtre du Rond-Point in the centre of Paris. Jacqueline Maillan, a popular comic actress for whom he had written it, was in the central role and Michel Piccoli played her brother. At the Théâtre des Amandiers his translation of *A Winter's Tale* was directed by Luc Bondy. In the metro, Koltès was struck by police 'wanted' posters with photos of the murderer Roberto Succo and became interested in his case, especially after he had seen television pictures of Succo's last hours on the roof-top of an Italian prison.

1989 Death of Koltès in Paris a week after his forty-first birthday (15th April). Shortly before his death, he had completed his final play *Roberto Zucco*.

1990 World première of *Roberto Zucco*, directed by Peter Stein at the Berlin Schaubühne.

1997   Publication of *Plays I* by Methuen, comprising *Black Battles with Dogs* (trs. D. Bradby and M. Delgado); *Return to the Desert* (trs. D. Bradby); *Roberto Zucco* (trs. M. Crimp). First British performance of *Roberto Zucco* at the Royal Shakespeare Company at The Other Place, Stratford, directed by James MacDonald.

Chronology of plays – premières/publications (from a list by Serge Saada published in *Alternatives Théâtrales*, 35–36 June 1990).

Les Amertumes adapted from Gorki's novel *Childhood*, produced by the author, Strasbourg, 1970.

La Marche inspited by the Song of Songs, produced by the author, Strasbourg, 1971.

Procès Ivre inspired by Dostoievski's novel *Crime and Punishment*, produced by the author, Strasbourg, 1971.

L'Héritage, produced on Radio-France Alsace and then again on France-Culture (also Radio), 1972.

Récits Morts, produced by the author, Strasbourg, 1973.

Des Voix sourdes, produced on Radio-France, Alsace and on France-Culture, 1974.

Le Jour de meurtres dans l'histoire d'Hamlet, 1974.

Sallinger inspired by the stories of J.D. Salinger, produced by Bruno Boeglin, Lyon, 1977. Published by Minuit, 1995.

La Nuit juste avant les forêts monologue, produced by the author, Avignon Festival, 1977. Published by Stock/Théâtre Ouvert, 1980; Minuit, 1988. First English production as *Twilight Zone*, directed by Pierre Audi, Edinburgh Festival and Almeida Theatre, 1981.

Combat de nègre et de chiens published by Stock/Théâtre Ouvert, 1980; Minuit, 1989. First produced by Françoise Kourilsky, La Mamma theatre, New York, 1982 in a translation by Matthew Ward; first French production by Patrice Chéreau, Théâtre des Amandiers, Nanterre, 1983.

8   In the Solitude of Cotton Fields

First English production as *Struggle of the Black Man and the Dogs*, directed by Michael Batz, Gate Theatre, 1988. English publication: *Struggle of the Dogs and the Black* (trans. Matthew Ward) in *New French Plays*, Methuen, 1989. New English translation: *Black Battles with Dogs* (trans. David Bradby and Maria Delgado) in *Plays I*, Methuen, 1997.

Le Lien du sang translation of *The Blood Knot* by Athol Fugard, first produced by Yutaka Wada, Avignon Festival, 1982.

Quai ouest published by Minuit, 1985. First produced by Stephane Stroux in a Dutch translation, Amsterdam, 1985; first French production by Patrice Chéreau, Théâtre des Amandiers, 1986.

Tabataba produced by Hammou Graia, Avignon Festival, 1986. Published by Minuit with *Roberto Zucco* (see below).

Dans la solitude des champs de coton published by Minuit, 1986. First produced by Patrice Chéreau, Théâtre des Amandiers, 1987.

Le Conte d'hiver translation of A *Winter's Tale* by Shakespeare, first produced by Luc Bondy, Théâtre des Amandiers, 1988. Published by Minuit, 1988.

Le Retour au désert, first produced by Patrice Chéreau, Théâtre du Rond-Point, Paris, 1988. Published by Minuit, 1988. In English: *Return to the Desert* (trans. David Bradby) in *Plays I*, Methuen, 1997.

Roberto Zucco, first produced by Peter Stein in a German translation by Simon Werle, Schaubühne, Berlin, 1990; first French production by Bruno Boeglin, Théâtre National Populaire, Villeurbanne, 1991. Published by Minuit, with *Tabataba*, 1990. in English: *Roberto Zucco* (trans. Martin Crimp) in *Plays I*, Methuen, 1997. First English production, directed by James MacDonald, The Other Place, Stratford, November 1997.

Extracted from David Bradby's Chronology to
Bernard-Marie Koltès Plays: 1.
Published by Methuen Drama in 1997.

Introduction

When Bernard-Marie-Koltès (b. 1948) died in 1989, he was already being hailed within European theatre circles as one of the most significant figures in French post-war theatre. This was partly to do with the fact that France's pre-eminent director, Patrice Chéreau, chose to stage most of the plays he wrote in the 1980s. Two years after being appointed artistic director of Nanterre's Théâtre des Amandiers, Chéreau spoke of a crisis in the French theatre which was, in his view, crippled by a lack of 'great playwrights'. 'There are many people who write plays', he went on to state, 'but I don't know of anyone who knows how to use language dramatically, to incorporate it into a theatrical discourse. One of my primary goals at Nanterre is to search out and nurture young playwrights like Bernard-Marie Koltès'.

In the Solitude of Cotton Fields was first published in 1986 and then staged by Chéreau the following year at Nanterre. The play is a beautiful, bleak dissection of an enigmatic encounter between two men and offers a fascinating and discomforting vision of the concerns of Western society on the cusp of chaos. We never learn the men's names; they are simply referred to as The Dealer and The Client. The Dealer (who Koltès had initially insisted ought to be black) has something to sell, but we never learn exactly what this is. The Client appears seems to have come with the intent of buying some item or other but the precise nature of his desire is never revealed. The deal (rather than love or romance) is the basis for the negotiation of relationships between these characters. Neither character appears to know what the other wants from him and the whole play functions as an investigation of the momentary split-second glance which brings them together. Each is subtly differentiated. The Client, offering a measured study in rationality, dreaded cordiality, desired impenetrability, and despised ambiguity, seeks security in the artifice of a world of electric lights and air-conditioning – a sharp contrast to the shuffling Dealer with his fear of lifts. Meeting at an unspecified time and place, each refuses to reveal exactly what it is they want. The Dealer looks to divine the desire of

The Client, questioning and undermining all The Client's absolutes, but The Client refuses to allow him a way in, so we never really learn what The Dealer is offering him. It is the conversation of two insiders listened to by an audience who don't understand their language and don't necessarily know what exactly is going on. Rather than a story, *Solitude* is the grounds for meeting in a world where love appears conspicuously absent. The journey both men embark on carries the play forward and the games they play through a manipulation of language sets up a series of traps which each attempts not to fall into.

An erotic undercurrent pulls The Dealer and The Client together whilst fear appears to push them apart. The arguments employed are vicious, intense, and seductive. Interest is consistently maintained through a discursive battle which intrigues, amuses and frustrates. The men's accelerating battle, lurching from the ordinary to the extravagant, transgressing genres, tones and moods, seeps into the theatrical space with alarming vigour. Human interaction is here shown to be nothing more than a deal, an elusive transaction in a society of uneasy alliances where everything is up for negotiation and bartering is a way of life.

Revealing human alienation within a violent urban landscape, Koltès creates a brutalised world, both frighteningly real and profoundly mythical. For Koltès, the stage was a fictional place where he could create encounters between individuals who might not normally meet in real life. *Solitude* is in many ways Koltès's core work in that it offers a stark, pared down verbal combat between opposing ideologies in the form of a duel. If actors and directors have found Koltès's work a challenge it is precisely because of the ambiguous nature of the stage directions which refuse to specifically pin the action down and an antipathy to the kind of character realism which is habitually associated with method acting. Total psychological identification with a role is pretty much impossible in Koltès. The rhythmical formulations and linguistic dexterity of his language prevent easy identification or empathy. The challenge for actors, director and audience lies in acknowledging that much in Koltès is left unsaid.

Koltès doesn't ask 'why' things happen but 'how' actions are carried out. It is on this subtle difference that Koltès's work hinges and it is this characteristic which renders him a significant dramatic innovator. Like Beckett before him, Koltès shatters all the codes governing the way plays are constructed. When Benedict Nightingale reviewed *Solitude* at the Almeida in 1990 he made the observation that Koltès is 'The kind of European intellectual that makes Englishmen very nervous indeed'. His writing is distant from our own theatrical traditions of contemporary playwriting. Moving away from the reaffirmative tendencies of the classic realist text, *Solitude* refuses to furnish actors or audiences with safe, easy or sentimental answers. Nothing can be taken for granted in Koltès's writing and this creates veritable challenges for audiences who like clear decisive narratives or subjects which appear to have direct relevancy to their lives. Koltès, like Marivaux before him, consciously plays with language, forging dramatic fusions of the banal and the sublime and infusing his dark dramatic pieces with philosophical meditations and dissections of desire, obsession, and power. *Solitude* places the dramatic characters in a compressed situation from whence there is no escape. Class and gender come into play to reveal tortured domestic relations which reverberate across the wider political and social strata.

Convinced, like Chekhov that his plays were comic, Koltès places central emphasis on marginal unsympathetic characters who have a forever uneasy presence in the shattered and disturbing corners that his plays illuminate. The intense dialogue that he constructs in all his works is carefully worked from the idiom of ordinary speech with a charged tension that is established between the dialogue and the situation or environment in which it takes place. Language functions as a weapon, used and abused mercilessly by characters as they seek to establish their territory. Each of the characters fights with dialogue that attempts to change or affect or seduce the other through the multiple and many-layered deals that are being negotiated. Koltès stands alongside Samuel Beckett and Jean Genet in his radical refashioning of theatrical language. This has posed veritable challenges to translators who have faced difficult decisions in rendering his meticulously structured language – *Solitude* is constructed like a musical fugue – into an workable English idiom. This translation provides a welcome reminder of the importance of a dramatist whose works, embracing themes like multiculturalism, the growing allure of violence, the construction of sexual and cultural identities, the deceptive nature of language, the breakdown of communication and the overriding fact that anything can be bought and sold if the price is right, boldly reflect the problematic prisms of late twentieth century society.

Maria M. Delgado
Reader in Drama and Theatre Arts at Queen Mary
The University of London

A deal *is the commercial transaction of some valuable, prohibited or strictly controlled, in neutral, unspecified territory, not set aside for the purpose, between he who purveys and he who has to have, and conducted by tacit agreement, convention, or double meaning – with the aim of avoiding the risk of betrayal or swindle that such operations involve – at any hour of day or night, outside regular opening hours and off business premises, usually indeed during the very hours such premises are closed.*

Characters

The Dealer
The Client

The Dealer   If you are out walking at this hour and in
this place, you must want something, and that something
I'm sure I may help you with; because I was here on this
spot long before you came by, and will be here long after
you've gone, not even the savage grapplings of man and
beast that occur at this hour scare me away, and that's
because I've got what those who pass by here want, which is
like carrying a weight you have to unload on whoever does
pass, be they man or beast.

That's why I'm approaching you, despite its being the hour
when, ordinarily, man and beast are falling savagely one
upon another, why I am approaching you, look, hands out
in the open, palms towards you, with all the humility
someone with something to offer shows towards someone
who might buy, with all the humility of someone who has
something towards someone who might want something;
and I see that you do want something, just like seeing a light
go on, high up in a building, at dusk; I'm approaching you
just the way the dusk approaches that first light, slowly,
respectfully, almost affectionately, leaving beast and man far
below in the street, straining at the leash and baring their
teeth so savagely.

Not that I discern as yet what it is you might want, nor am I
in any hurry to find out; since the want a buyer has is the
most melancholic of things, let's look upon it as a little
secret, begging to be penetrated yet with which we take our
time; or like a present which comes all wrapped up, yet still
we take our time before unfastening the string. But the point
is I myself have wanted, for as long as I've been in this
place, all that every man or beast might want at this dark
hour, which drags them from their homes despite the savage
squealing of beasts unsatisfied and men unsatisfied; that's
why I know, better than the anxious buyer who, for a while,
keeps some mystery about him, like a young virgin bred to
be a whore, that whatever you're going to ask me for I have,
and that you only have – without feeling wounded by any of
that vague sense of injustice that he who asks does feel at the
hands of he who offers – to ask it of me.

Since the only true injustice on this earth is the injustice of the earth itself, barren through cold, barren through heat, rarely rendered bountiful by heat and cold acting gently together; then there's no injustice in being forever on the same patch of earth, subject to the same cold or to the same heat or to the two acting gently together, and every man or beast who can look another man or beast in the eye is his equal for they walk the same fine, flat line, the same level of latitude, are slaves to the same colds and the same heats, rich in the same way and poor in the same way; and the only borderline that truly exists is the one between he who buys and he who sells, and that is blurred, since both possess the want and the thing they want, both empty and at the same time served to the full, yet with no more of injustice than there is in being male or female among men or beasts. That's why, for now, I borrow humility and lend you arrogance, so we can be told apart at this hour which is inescapably the same for you and for me.

So tell me, my melancholy virgin, at this very moment when men and beasts are squealing sotto voce, tell me what it is you want that I can supply, and I will supply it, gently, almost respectfully, perhaps with some affection; then, having filled in what's empty and smoothed out what swells in us, we will take our leave of each other, balanced nicely on our fine line of latitude, satisfied amid men and beasts, dissatisfied with being men and beasts; but don't ask me to discern what it is you want, for then I'd have to enumerate everything I've got to satisfy all who pass by here all the time that I'm here, and the time needed for such an enumeration would dry my heart and doubtless exhaust your hope.

The Client   I'm not out walking in this particular place at this particular hour; I'm out walking, full stop, on my way from one point to another, about my own business which has to do with those two points and not with anywhere in between; I don't know anything about dusk, or any of this I might be 'wanting' and don't wish to be bothered with anything along the way. I was going from that lighted

window up there behind me to that lighted window over
there in front of me in a straight line which happens across
you only because you've deliberately placed yourself there.
There isn't any way one can get from up there to up there
without having to come down and then go back up, two
movements which, absurdly, cancel each other out and
carry the risk, at every step, of treading in some waste
thrown from the windows; the higher one lives the more
wholesome it is, and the harder it gets to come down; so
when the lift deposits you here you're condemned to set foot
among everything they didn't want up there, piles of
decomposing memories, like in a restaurant when the waiter
makes out the bill and you feel sick listening to him
enumerate all the dishes that are even now rotting-down
deep inside you.

Now, had the darkness been thicker than this, such that I
couldn't see your face; then, perhaps, I could have been
mistaken as to exactly what you are up to here and why
you've stepped out of your way to set yourself across my
path, and I, in my turn could have stepped aside and given
way; but how dark would it have to be to make you appear
less dark than the darkness itself? There is no moonless
night that won't seem like midday if that's when you happen
to be out for a stroll, and that midday will show you that it's
not the chance of where a lift opens which sets you here, but
some inscrutable law of gravity, which applies only to you,
which you wear, as visibly as if a sack were lashed to your
shoulders, tying you to this hour, and to this place where
you sit and sigh and calculate how high the buildings are.

As for what I want, if it were something I could remember
now, here in the dusk, amid the squealing of beasts – of
which, by the way, there's not so much as the tip of a tail to
be seen – other than the immediate want I have to see you
drop the humility and keep the arrogance – for if I do have
some weakness for arrogance, I loathe humility, in me and
in others, so it's an exchange I'd scarcely be pleased with –
whatever it might be I do want, you would certainly not
have it. What I want, if it is one thing, and if I were to set it

before you, would scorch your face, have you fall back screaming, hands up to protect yourself, and you'd be off back into the dark like a dog with its tail so far between its legs you'd think it'd been cut off. But no, the confusion of this place and this hour makes me forget whether I have ever wanted anything that I can recall; no, I don't have anything to offer you save the chance to step aside so I don't have to do anything, that you remove yourself from the route I'm following, that you cancel yourself out, since the light, up there, near the top of the building, nearly in darkness, shines on whatever, piercing the dark like a lit match pierces the cloth which seeks to smother it.

The Dealer   You're right to assume I'm not from up there and that I have no intention of making it up there, but you would be wrong if you believed that mortifies me. I avoid lifts like a dog avoids water. Not that they refuse to open their doors to me, nor do I loathe having them close their doors behind me; but lifts in motion give me a tickly feeling, I lose my dignity in them; and though I like being tickled, I also like to be able not to be when my dignity requires it. It's the same with lifts as with some drugs, using them too much leaves you between, never up never down, taking curved lines for straight lines, finding ice inside fire. However, from all the time I've spent on this spot, I know how to recognise those flames which, far off, behind the windows, seem frozen like winter dusk, but which you only have to approach gently, perhaps affectionately, remembering that their gleam is not so utterly cold, and what I seek is not to snuff you out, but to shelter you from the wind, and dry the dampness of the hour with the warmth from that flame.

For, whatever you say, the line you were walking along, straight as perhaps it was, did bear off when you spied me, and I grasped that precise moment when your path veered, veered not to avoid me, but so as to come towards me, otherwise we would never have met, you would have missed me by miles, cracking on like someone does who's bent only on getting from one place to another; and I would never have caught you since I only get about so slowly, quietly, almost without moving at all, just the shuffle of someone who's not on his way from one place to another but who stays in one place, lies in wait for whoever passes and for them to adjust their course just a little bit. And if I say that you did veer, and if you're going to insist that it was in order to avoid me, and in reply I insist that it was to bring you closer, this is because in the end you've not really deviated at all, because every straight line only exists in relation to one plan, but we move according to two different plans, and that in the end there's only the one fact: your eye fell my way and I intercepted it, or the reverse, and that however firmly you set off, the line along which you were travelling became relative, complex, neither straight nor curved, but fated.

The Client   Nevertheless, I don't have to want something illicit, just to please you. I conduct my business during regular hours, in places approved and under electric light. For all you know I might very well be a whore, but if I am my brothel isn't part of the world down here; it's out in the open, above board, closes its doors in the evening, has certificates framed on the wall and is lit by electricity, for you can't guarantee sunlight, however well it treats us. What do you expect of a man whose every step is regular, lawful, double-stamped and whose every closet is flooded with electric light? And suppose I am, just going along, now held up, suspended, displaced, off-side, out of life, on remand, absent for all practical purposes, not all there, so to speak – does one say when a man's crossing the Atlantic by plane that at that very moment he's over Greenland ? or that at that very moment he's down in the drink? – and, if I did step out of my way, if the straight line between the point I'm coming from and the point I'm going to which may not be right, indeed not right at all, suddenly bears off, it's because you are barring the way, full of illicit intent and presumptions of illicit intent on my part. So here's what in all the world I do loathe, even more than illicit intent, more than an illicit act itself: it's the look in the eye of someone who presumes you full of illicit intentions and familiar with such intentions; and not only that eye itself, which would stir a mountain torrent – like yours, raise a cloud in a glass of clear water – but because just the weight of that eye makes me feel as though the virginity in me is suddenly violated, my innocence turned to guilt, and that straight line that was supposed to lead me from one point of light to another point of light has, because of you, become ravelled, a dark labyrinth in the dark territory where I've lost myself.

The Dealer   You're trying to slip a thorn under my horse's saddle so he'll twitch and bolt; but though my horse is nervous sometimes and not so biddable, if he's kept on a tight rein he won't bolt that easily; a thorn's not a razor blade, he knows how thick leather is, and what pricks he can get used to. Even so, who knows everything about the moods of horses? Sometimes they'll stand a needle driven into their flank, other times a speck of dust on the harness can make them rear, twist round on themselves and throw their rider.

So please, not that; if I'm speaking to you, at this hour, and gently, perhaps still with respect, it is not the same with you: you can't help it, but the way you're talking gets you noticed as someone in fear, just a little, but sharp enough, against all reason, but there for all to see, like a small child expecting a smacking from his father; now the way I talk doesn't get me noticed, it's how people do talk down here and at this time of night with men straining at the leash and pigs butting their heads against the rails of their pen; I keep hold of my tongue the same way you hang on to the bridle of a stallion so he doesn't throw himself on the mare, for if I released the pressure of my fingers, unflexed my arms one little bit, my words would throw me, hurl me up to the horizon, with all the violence of an Arab horse who senses the desert and can be held back no longer.

That's why, without knowing you, I've treated you well from the first word I spoke, from the first step I took towards you, a correct step, humble, respectful, without knowing what it might be about you that merited such respect, without knowing anything about you which could make me know whether a comparison of our two conditions would justify that I be humble and you be arrogant, allowing you that arrogance because it was dusk as we were approaching each other, the hour when correctness is no longer obligatory and thus becomes indispensable, when only a savage encounter in the dark is obligatory, and I would have been able to fall upon you like a cloth on a candle flame, been able to seize you by the shirt neck and take you by surprise. And this correctness that I've offered you, indispensable, but for free, does bind you to me, if only because I would have been able, just out of pride, to boot you like you boot a can in the gutter, because I knew that the first difference between us is size – and size in this place and at this hour makes all the difference – and we both know who's the boot and who's the can.

The Client   Even if it is what I did, you must know that I would not have wanted to meet your eye. Out for a stroll, the eye rests here and there and believes itself on safe, neutral ground, like a bee in a field of flowers, or a cow's muzzle in a well-fenced meadow. But how are we to deal with what it meets? Looking up into the sky makes me feel nostalgic, staring at the earth saddens me, what we regret and what we merely remember are equally unbearable. So one must keep the eye straight ahead, on one's own plane, wherever one's putting one's feet at the time; that's why when I was walking along there on my way to this moment and this spot where I'm now stopped, sooner or later my eye was bound to collide with whatever was set there or walking on the same plane as me; and, because of how distance and the laws of perspective work, every man and beast is, provisionally and approximately, on the same plane as me. Perhaps, in effect, the only thing left to distinguish us, the only injustice, if you prefer, is that which makes one feel vaguely more in fear of a smacking than the other; and that the only resemblance, or justice if you prefer, is ignorance of the degree to which this fear is shared, the degree of the future likelihood of such a smacking, and their respective degree of violence.

So, are we doing anything other than rehearsing the usual encounters of man with beast and beasts with other beasts in hours and places illicit and shadowy and of interest not to law or electricity? And this is why, out of hatred of beasts and hatred of men, I prefer law and I prefer electric light, and indeed I have good reason to believe that all natural light, all unfiltered air and seasonal temperatures unregulated make the world hazardous; for there's nothing peaceable, nor lawful in the elements of nature, there's nothing businesslike in illicit business, there's only threat, flight, boot and fist; without something to sell and something to buy and without a currency that's viable and a list of prices, only shadows, shadows of men accosting one another in the night; and if you accosted me because in the end you want to put the boot in; and if I ask why you want to put the boot in, I know you would reply that that's your secret, and there's no need for me to know why. So I'll not ask you anything. Does one speak to a rooftile that's slithering down and about to shatter your skull? One is like a bee clinging to a sick flower, like the muzzle of a cow wanting to graze on the other side of the electric fence; you keep quiet or you run away, you regret, you wait, you do what you can, without rhyme or reason, outside the law, in the dark.

I've set foot in the farmyard and the squelch of mysteries is like the shit in the gutter; and from these mysteries and this darkness of yours, comes the rule that states that whenever two men meet each other one must always choose to strike first; and without doubt, at this hour and in places like this if any man or beast met your eye one would have to approach him, strike him and then say: I don't know if you meant to strike me, but, if you did, for some reason that's mysterious and beyond reason, and which you would not have believed it necessary to acquaint me with, however that might be, I preferred to strike first, and my reason, even though beyond reason, is at least not secret: it's because through my happening to be here, you happen to be here, there was that accidental meeting of our eyes, the possibility that you might strike me first, and I preferred to be the tile slithering off the roof rather than the skull, the electric fence rather than the cow's bare nose.

Except, if you really are a salesman with merchandise which you won't unveil and which I don't have any means of discerning, and I a buyer who wants something so secret that I don't know what it is myself and have to scratch my memory like you scratch a scab to make it bleed, if that is true, why do you still keep your merchandise under wraps when I've halted here and I'm waiting, keep everything sealed up in that big sack you're carrying, lashed to your shoulders, impalpable as the law of gravity, without existence, only coming into being when married to the form of a want; like a tout in front of a strip joint, who takes you by the elbow on your way home, and slips into your ear: she's in tonight? Whereas, if you would show it all to me, would name what it is you have to offer, licit, illicit or whatever, but named at least, and hence open to evaluation, then I'd know how to say no, and not feel any longer like a tree bent by a wind that's coming from nowhere and shaking it by the roots. For I know how to say no and I like to say no, I am capable of dazzling you with all the ways I have of saying no, of making you see just how many ways there are to say no, beginning with all the ways there are to say yes, like those prickteasers who try on blouse after blouse and shoe after shoe just so as not to buy a single one of them, the pleasure they take in trying them all is consummated by the pleasure they take in turning them all down. So decide, show yourself: are you the thug kicking a can in the gutter or are you a proper salesman? If you're the latter, spread out your merchandise first, and one will stop to look at them.

The Dealer   It's because I want to be a salesman, not a thug, but a true salesman, that I don't tell you what I've got and what I have to offer you, because I don't want to endure a refusal which is the one thing that everyone who sells something dreads above all, because it is the one weapon he does not have at his own disposal. Thus I have never learned to say no, and I don't in the least wish to learn how to say no; every kind of way to say yes, those I do know: yes wait a moment, yes wait a while, yes wait here with me for all eternity; yes I do have it, yes I will have it, yes I did have it and I'll have it in again soon, no I never did have it but I will get it for you. Suppose somebody comes up to speak to me: he wants something, confesses what it is, would you say no, you haven't got whatever it is he wants? I'll say yes, I've got whatever it is he wants; if he then says, are you just making out that you've got it? even when I am, I always have it. And if he says, look, in the end you don't really have a clue what I'm after, do you? even then, despite all that, I've still got the necessary.

But the more correct the salesman, the more perverse the buyer; every salesman is looking to satisfy some want he doesn't yet know, while the buyer always subordinates what he wants to the primary satisfaction, which is to turn down what he's offered; thus the want he's not confessed to is exalted by his refusal, and he forgets what it is he wants in the pleasure of humiliating the salesman. But I'm not one of those salesmen who'll change tack just to suit the clients' taste for anger and indignation. I'm not here to give pleasure, but to fill the abyss of want, to recall what that want is, to give it a name, lead it out into the open, give it form and weight, with all the necessary cruelty there is in giving form and weight to want. And because I see what you want appearing like saliva at the corner of your mouth, though you lick it back, I'll wait for it to start running down your chin, or for you to be drooling on the floor before I offer you a handkerchief, because if I offer you one too soon, I know you'll refuse it, and that is a pain I don't want to bear.

For what every man or beast dreads at this hour when man is on a level with the beast and every beast on a level with every man, is not pain, for pain balances out, the capacity to inflict and to tolerate pain balances out; what he dreads above all else is pain that is strange to him, of being brought

to endure pain that is not familiar. Thus, the distance there
will always be in the world between the brute on the one
hand and the young girl on the other, comes not from the
evaluation of the respective force at their command, if that
were so the world would be sorted very simply between
brutes and girls, brute would fall upon girl and the world
would be simple; no, what holds the brute back from the
girl, and will do so for all time, is the infinite mystery, and
the infinite strangeness of weapons, those little canisters they
carry in their handbags for instance that squirt stuff into the
eyes of brutes so suddenly there they are crying in front of
the girls, all dignity snuffed, no longer a man or beast, just
tears of shame falling into the earth of some field. That's
why the brute and the young girl fear and mistrust one
another as much as anything, because one can only inflict
the pain one can bear oneself, and only fear the pain one is
not capable of inflicting oneself.

So, I beg you, don't refuse to tell me what it is you want so
much, for which you've let your eye meet mine; if it's a
matter of not wounding your dignity the least little bit, well,
speak it as though you were speaking to a tree, or facing the
wall of a prison, or in the solitude of a cotton field where
you are out walking, naked, at night; tell me without
meeting my eye. For the only true cruelty of dusk, of this
hour where we both now stand, is not that one man might
wound the other, or mutilate him, torture him, tear head
and limb apart, or even make him cry; the true, terrible
cruelty is the one by which some man or beast cuts the other
off, like dot . . . dot . . . dot in the middle of a sentence, or,
having first met his eye, then turns away, as though that had
been a mistake, like having just started a letter and then
screwing it up after writing no more than the date.

The Client   You're a strange sort of rogue, you steal
nothing or you leave it too late to steal anything, a robber
who slips over the wall into the orchard at night, shakes the
trees and leaves without picking up the fruit – most
eccentric. But you're the one who's familiar with these
places and I'm the stranger here; I'm the one who's

frightened and with good reason to be frightened; I'm the one who doesn't know you, who can't know you, who can only just make out your silhouette in the dark. It was up to you to discern what's what, name what you've got, and then, perhaps with a nod of the head, or some other sign you'd recognise, I would have said yes; but I've no wish for what I want to be spilled out for nothing like blood on foreign soil. You're not risking anything; in me you see anxiety, hesitation, mistrust; you know where I've come from and where I'm going; you know these streets, you know this hour of the night, you know what your plans are; I know nothing and I'm risking everything. Facing you is like facing men who dress like women dressing like men, in the end, you don't know what sex you're looking at.

You laid your hand on me like the rogue on his victim, or like the law on the cutpurse, and ever since I've been in pain, not knowing anything, not what my fate's to be, whether I'm the accused or just an accomplice, what I'm in pain for, or what kind of wound you're making or where my own blood's flowing from. But perhaps, in truth, it's not that you're at all strange, just cunning; perhaps you're some plod sent out undercover, a *provocateur*, perhaps, in the end, you're a more upstanding citizen than I am. And hey presto, for nothing, by accident, without my having said anything or wanted anything, because I didn't know who you are, because I'm a stranger who doesn't know the language or the customs, what's proper or improper, the wrong side or the right side, and who acts dazzled, lost, it comes to look as though it was me who asked you for something, as if I'd asked you for the worst thing imaginable and that I will be pronounced guilty for having asked for it. A want that's like blood flowing out of me round your feet, a want I don't know and don't recognise, that only you know, and that you are the judge of.

If that's how it is, if all this is a sly effort to betray me, to drive me into acting with you or against you so that in either case I'll be guilty, if that's how it is, then at least recognise that I have not acted in any way either with you or against you, that there's nothing for me to be reproached for, that I've remained honest every instant till now. Be my witness that I was not pleased to be here in the dark where you've stopped me, that I only stopped here because you put your hand on mine; be my witness that I called for light, that I didn't slip out into the dark like a thief, of my own free will and full of illicit intent, but that I was surprised and that I cried out, like an infant in its cradle when, all of a sudden, the night-light goes out.

The Dealer   If you believe I've got violent designs upon you – and perhaps you're right – don't jump to conclusions about the kind of violence, or the label to stick on it. You were born with the notion that a man's sex keeps itself hidden in one particular spot and stays there, and it's a notion you cling to carefully; however, I know – though I was born just the same way you were – that a man's sex, after a passage of time that he spends waiting and forgetting, in solitude, moves gently elsewhere, never hidden in one particular spot, sometimes in view, then where one doesn't expect; and no sex, after a passage of time where a man has learned to sit and rest quietly in solitude, resembles any other sex any more than male sex resembles female sex; that it is absolutely not male disguised as female, but a gentle hesitation between, like the shift between seasons, neither summer in the guise of winter, nor winter in the guise of summer.

Nevertheless, it's not worth panicking over suppositions; one has to keep hold of one's imagination just as one must keep hold of one's young fiancée: if it's good to see her roam, it's silly to let her lose all sense of propriety. I'm not cunning, only curious; I put my hand on your arm out of pure curiosity, to know whether flesh which has the appearance of a plucked chicken feels warm like a live chicken or cold like a dead chicken, and now I know. The pain you feel, if I might say this without offence, is the same chill a live, half-plucked chicken feels, ailing, moth-eaten in the strict sense of the term; when I was little I used to run after chickens in the backyard so that I could feel them in my hands and find out, purely from curiosity, if their temperature was that of the living or the dead. Today as I touched you I felt the chill of death, but I also felt your pain from the cold, pain only the living can feel. That's why I tendered you my jacket to cover your shoulders, since I don't feel pain from the cold. I've never felt it, indeed what I have felt is the pain of not knowing that kind of pain, so that the only dream I used to have when I was little – one of those dreams that are not of the future, free and clear, but of prison after prison, that moment when an infant perceives the bars of his first prison, when those who are born of slaves dream they are the sons of masters – my dream was that I would know snow and ice, know the cold which is your pain.

If it's only my jacket I've lent you, that isn't because I don't realise that you feel the cold elsewhere than in your top half, but, if I might say so without giving offence, from top to toe and even a bit beyond those extremities; and, indeed, I've always thought that one must give someone who's feeling the chill that piece of clothing for wherever they are feeling it, even at the risk of finding oneself naked, top to toe, and perhaps a bit beyond those extremities; but my mother, who wasn't at all niggardly, but did have a sense of propriety, told me that while it was commendable to give away your shirt or jacket or any other garment for the top half of the body, you have to think a long while before you give away your shoes, and never, in any circumstances, is it proper to give away your trousers.

So, just as I know – without explaining it to myself with absolute certitude – that the earth on which you and I and everyone else are set is itself balanced on the horn of a bull and is kept in that position by the hand of providence, so I try, without knowing why but without the least hesitation, to stay within the limits of what is proper, avoiding the improper just as a child knows it must avoid leaning over the edge of a roof even before it has understood anything about the laws of falling bodies. And just as the child believes the reason he's told not to lean over the edge of a roof is to prevent him from flying, for a long time I believed that a boy was told not to give away his trousers so as to prevent him from unveiling the ardour, or the languor, of his feelings. But now I understand things better, and I recognise better those things that I don't understand, that here I am in this place at this hour for such and such a time, that I've seen such and such a number of passers-by pass by, that I've met their eye and, such and such a number of times, put my hand on their arm, without understanding anything and without wanting to understand, but yet without forsaking meeting their eye and putting my hand on their arm – it is, by the way, easier to catch a man passing by than it is a chicken in a backyard – and I now know very well that there is nothing improper in ardour or languor that must be hidden, and that it's necessary to follow the rules without knowing why.

Moreover, if I might say so without giving offence, I hoped, in covering your shoulders with my jacket, to make you seem more familiar to me. Too much strangeness can make me shy, and, seeing you coming towards me so swiftly, I asked myself why a man, who is not sick, is dressed like some moulting, moth-eaten chicken walking about the backyard with an ailment that makes its feathers stick this way and that; and without any doubt, out of shyness I should have been content to scratch my head and step aside to avoid you had I not seen, as your eye met mine, the gleam there of somebody who is about to, in the strict sense of the term, ask for something, and that gleam made me ignore your get-up.

The Client   What do you hope to get from me? Every move I think will be a blow ends up as a caress; it's very unnerving to be caressed when one expects to be hit. I must insist that at least you take more care if you want me to linger. Since you claim to be selling me something only by chance, why didn't you check first whether I've got the wherewithal to pay? my pockets may be empty; it would have been reasonable to ask me to put my money down on the counter straightaway, just as with any other dubious client. You've not asked any such thing: what pleasure do you get from the risk of being ripped off? I've not come here for gentleness; gentleness works bit by bit, cuts up piece by piece, like they do a corpse in the anatomy theatre. I need my whole being; at least malice will keep me in one piece. So come on, get angry: or where will I draw my strength from? Get angry: then we'll stick to what we're about, and know we're both dealing with the same thing. If I do understand where I get my pleasure from, I don't understand where you get yours.

The Dealer   Had I doubted for an instant that you had the wherewithal to afford what you've come looking for, I would have kept out of your way when you approached me. Only common tradesmen demand proof of their clients' solvency; fashionable stores are discerning and demand nothing, they don't lower themselves to enquire after the amount or the signature on the cheque. There are goods to sell and goods to buy and so the question never presents itself as to whether the buyer can afford them nor how long it will take him to make up his mind. So I'm patient because one doesn't want to offend a man as he's leaving when you know he's going to come back. An insult one cannot take back, but politeness one can, so it's better to be polite time and again than to be rude even once. That's why I still won't get angry, because I have the time not to get angry, as well as the time to do so, and perhaps I will get angry when all this time is up.

The Client   Suppose – for the sake of argument – I allowed that I had behaved arrogantly – but with no real desire to do so – only because you ordered me to behave that way when you approached me with some design of yours I still can't discern – I've no gift for discernment – and that's what's still keeping me here; or suppose – for the sake of argument – I said to you that what is keeping me here is uncertainty about my place in your design and what I get out of it. Given the strangeness of the hour and the strangeness of the place and the strangeness of your advance upon me, I should have come towards you, drawn in just the way a first movement holds as long as no counter-movement opposes it. What if I could not help approaching you? was carried not by my own will but by the same sort of attraction as draws princes to slum it in taverns, or the child down in secret into the cellar, the attraction of the tiny, solitary atom for the dark mass, so impassive, so deep in shadow? I would have come towards you, listening calmly to how softly my blood beats through my veins, wondering whether the softness would grow louder or halt altogether; I should have come slowly perhaps, but full of hope, stripped of any want that could be spoken, ready to be satisfied with whatever anyone would offer me, because whatever was offered would have been like something dropped into the furrow of a field so barren from neglect it cannot tell one falling grain from any other; ready to be satisfied by anything, given the strangeness of our approach towards each other, from far off I would have believed you were approaching me, from far off I would have had the impression that your eye was seeking mine; then, I would have approached you, I would have met your eye; I would have been close to you, expecting from you – too many things – too many things, not for you to discern, for I don't know myself, I don't know myself how to discern anything, but I was expecting from you both the taste of wanting, and the idea of wanting, the thing itself, the price and the satisfaction.

The Dealer   There's no shame in forgetting in the evening what you will remember in the morning; evening is the time for forgetfulness, confusion, of want so heated it vaporises. Nevertheless the morning does gather the evening up into a great cloud and hangs it over the bed, and it would be stupid not to anticipate in the evening the rain that will fall next morning. Suppose then, for the sake of argument, you were to tell me that for the moment you lack all desire to express what you want, whether from fatigue or forgetfulness or from wanting too much, which itself leads to forgetfulness, then, for the sake of the other side of the argument, I would tell you not to tire yourself out any further but to borrow the want someone else has. Want can be stolen but it can't be invented; a jacket keeps one man as warm as another and want lends itself as readily as a piece of clothing. Since I must sell at any price and since you must buy at any price, well then, buy for whoever – it doesn't matter what exerts the pull that you latch on to, it will make the deal – buy, for example, to delight and satisfy whoever it is wakes in your sheets next to you, a nice little fiancée waking up will want something you've not yet got, but then you'll have the pleasure of offering it to her, and you'll be happy you have it because you will have bought it from me. It's the salesman's good fortune that so many different people exist, betrothed as they are to so many different goods in so many different ways, for the recollection of some of them takes turns with the recollection of others. And the merchandise that you are going to buy from me will do good service, and it doesn't matter for whom, if – for the sake of argument – you had no use for it.

The Client　The rules of engagement state that when one man meets another he finishes up nudging his shoulder and talking about women; the rules state that remembering women be the last recourse of exhausted combatants; the rules of engagement, your rules; I won't submit to them. I don't want any peace accord between us to come about in the absence of women, nor out of remembering that absence, nor out of any sort of remembering. Memories disgust me, and absent people disgust me too; I want to eat food no one has touched, not something already digested. I don't want any peace, no matter what it comes out of; I don't want any peace whoever finds it.

When a dog looks about him he only sees a dog world. In the same way, you make out that the world on which you and I stand is held on the tip of the horn of a bull by the hand of providence; but I know that it floats on the backs of three whales; that there is no providence at all, no equilibrium, only the caprice of three mindless monsters. Our worlds are therefore not the same, and our strangeness is as mixed into our nature as is the grape into wine. No, I won't lift a paw face to face with you, in the same place as you; I'm not drawn by the same gravity as you; I'm not born of the same female as you. It's not in the mornings that I wake and I don't sleep in sheets.

The Dealer   Don't get angry, squire, don't get angry. I'm only a poor salesman who knows nothing beyond this pitch where all I do is wait to sell something, who only knows what his mother taught him; and since she knew nothing, or almost nothing, I don't know anything either, or not much. But a good salesman does try to say what the buyer wants to hear, and in trying to discern what that is, he has to nose and lick here and there to see if there's a smell he can recognise. The smell you have about you wasn't a bit familiar, we're definitely not from the same mother. But to be able to approach you, I did suppose that you came from some mother, just like I did, that your mother made you some brothers, just like mine did, I don't know how many any more than you know how many hiccups you get after you've eaten a lot, but that, in any case, what does bring us together is that neither of us has much to distinguish us. And I caught hold of that, that at least we have that much in common, because one can travel a long way in the desert as long as there's something familiar to fix on. But if I've made a mistake, if you didn't come from a mother, and nobody made you any brothers, if you haven't a nice little fiancée who wakes up with you in the morning in your own sheets, then I beg your pardon squire.

Two men who cross paths have no other choice but to hit out at each other, whether it's with the violence of enmity or the gentleness of fraternity. And if they choose in the end, in the desert place that is that hour, to bring to mind what is not there, from the past, or from a dream, or out of lack, it's because there is not more strangeness between them than they can face. Before mystery one must allow oneself to open, to unveil oneself completely so that the mystery is forced to unveil itself in turn. Memories are the secret weapons that a man still keeps when he is stripped; to be absolutely open obliges openness in return: the very final nakedness. There's neither glory nor confusion for me in this, but because you are unknown to me, and yet more unknown every moment, well then, just as I took off my jacket and tendered it to you, just as I put out my hands to show I have no weapons, whether I'm a dog and you're human, or I'm human and you're something else again, whatever race I might be and whatever race you might be, at least I am offering it for your consideration, I'm offering my nakedness, to let you touch, feel, get used to, just like a man lets himself be searched for weapons.

That's why what I'm offering, prudently, gravely, quietly, is that you look on me in friendship, because one makes a better deal under cover of familiarity. I'm not looking to trick you, and don't ask for anything you don't want to give. The only comradeship worth the trouble that comes along with it does not require that one act in a certain way, but that one does not act at all; I'm offering you the stillness, the boundless patience and the blind injustice of the friend. Because there is no justice between those who don't know each other, and no friendship between those who do know each other, there is no bridge without a ravine. My mother always told me that it is silly to refuse an umbrella when you know it's going to rain.

The Client I preferred you cunning to friendly. Friendship gives less away than treachery. If it had been feelings I needed I would have told you, I would have asked the price and paid it. But feelings are only traded like with like; this is a fake transaction with fake money, a poor man's transaction mimicking the real thing. Does one trade a sack of rice for a sack of rice? You've nothing to offer which is why you put your feelings out on the counter like a bad business gives you a discount so you can't complain about the stuff afterwards. As for me, I don't have any feelings to give you in return; I've not got any on me, never thought to bring any out, search me. So, keep your hand in your pocket, your mother in the bosom of your family and your memories for your solitude, that's the least you can do.

I will never want this familiarity between us that you're

trying to set up so stealthily. I didn't want your hand on my
arm, I didn't want your jacket, I didn't want the risk of
being mixed up with you. And be sure you take notice of
this: if a short while ago you were surprised by my
appearance, and you didn't care to hide your surprise, mine
was at least as great as I saw you approaching me. But, on
strange territory, the stranger seeks to hide his astonishment,
because for him everything bizarre just appears as local
custom, and he has to accommodate himself like he does to
the climate or the local dish. If I took you to my people, you
would be the stranger having to hide his astonishment, and
we'd be the natives, free to show it, all gathering round,
pointing at you, and in no time you'd be in a freak show
with everybody wanting to know where to buy tickets.

You're not here to do business. You're hanging around first
to beg and then to rob, first jaw-jaw then war. You're not
here to satisfy any want. I had wants, they fell all around us
and they've been trampled as you marked time here; the
big, the little, the complicated, the straightforward, all you
had to do was to stoop and gather them up in handfuls; but
you let them roll into the gutter, because you don't have
what it takes to satisfy even the little, even the
straightforward ones. You are poor and you're not out here
because you've a taste for it, but out of poverty, necessity
and ignorance. I don't make a show of buying pious images
or dropping coins in a hat for a few chords of pathetic
strumming. I give to charity if I want to give to charity,
otherwise I pay the asking price. Let the beggars beg, let
them dare to tender their hand, and let the robbers rob.

I'm not trying to insult you or please you; I don't want to be
good, or wicked, to strike or be struck, to seduce or for you
to try to seduce me. I want to be zero. I dread cordiality, I
have no vocation for cousinage, and, even more than the
violence of any blow, what I fear is the violence of
comradery. Let us both be zeros, both perfectly round,
impenetrable one to the other, side by side for a while, but
each rolling in his own direction. Now that we are alone in
the infinite solitude of this hour and this place, neither of

which is a definable hour, a definable place, because there is
no reason for my meeting you, nor for your crossing my
path, nor any reason for cordiality, nor any hidden code laid
down for us that makes sense and gives us a direction – let
us be simple, solitary and proud zeros.

The Dealer   But it's too late now: the account's been
drawn on and it has to balance. It's fair enough to rob
somebody who's tight and keeps everything under lock and
key for his own solitary pleasure, but it lacks refinement to
be stealing when everything's there to be bought and sold.
And although, for a while, it is permissible to carry a debt –
for a fair, agreed time – it's obscene to give and to accept
that one gives something for nothing. We are here to do
business, not fight a battle, so there shouldn't be a loser and
a winner. If you think you'll leave here with your pockets
bulging like some robber, you're forgetting the guard dog
down the street – he'll bite you in the arse.

Since you came down here, amidst the hostilities of men
and enraged beasts, in search of nothing you could put your
finger on, since you want to be damaged for who knows
what reason, it's going to be necessary, before you can turn
your back, for you to pay, to empty your pockets so that
there's nothing owed and nothing's been given away for
free. Don't trust merchants: a merchant robbed is more
jealous of his goods than a landlord looted: don't trust any
merchant, how they speak has the appearance of respect,
the appearance of gentleness, the appearance of humility,
the appearance of love, but only the appearance.

The Client   Then what is there that you've lost and I've
gained? for I might strip-search my memory and not find
anything I've gained. I'll pay what a thing really costs; but
I'm not paying for the wind, for the dark, for the void
between us. If you've lost something, if your personal
fortune is the lighter for meeting me, then where is this
something that eludes the both of us? Show me. No, I've
enjoyed nothing, and I'll pay for nothing.

The Dealer   If you want to know what's been put down

on your account right from the beginning, and which you'll
have to pay for before you turn your back on me, then let
me tell you it covers the expectation, and the patience, and
the recommendation of the goods to the client, and the hope
of selling, especially the hope, that which makes a debtor of
every man who approaches another with an eye that's
asking for something. Every promise to sell infers the
promise to buy, and there's a forfeit to pay for anyone who
breaks that promise.

The Client   We're not, you and I, alone, lost somewhere
out in the fields. If I called out from here towards that wall,
high up, towards the sky, you would see lights come on,
hear steps approaching, help coming. If it's hard to hate on
your own, when there's several of you it becomes a pleasure.
You take on men rather than women because you fear the
cries women make, you assume a man will feel ashamed to
cry out; you count on the dignity, the vanity, the muteness
of men. You can keep that kind of dignity. If you will me
any harm, I'll call, I'll cry out, I'll demand help, I'll have
you hear every way there is of calling for help for I know
them all.

The Dealer   So, if you don't find flight dishonourable
what's stopping you from fleeing? Flight is a subtle means of
combat; you are subtle; you should flee. You're like those fat
ladies in tea shops who slip between the tables and knock
over all the jugs: you carry your arse behind you like it's
something to be ashamed of, turning this way and that
trying to pretend it doesn't exist. However well you manage
it, you'll still get it bitten.

The Client   I'm not the kind that attacks first. I need
time. Perhaps, in the end, it would be better to search each
other for lice than bite each other. I need time. I don't want
to be the casualty of a mad dog. Come on, come with me;
let's look for some people, we're exhausted by solitude.

The Dealer   There's the jacket that you didn't take when
I tendered it to you, and now, you're going to have to bend
and pick it up.

The Client   If I did spit on something, I just spat, not at anything, on a piece of clothing; and if it did go in your direction, it wasn't meant for you, you didn't have to move to make sure it missed you; and if you do move so as to get it full in the face, because you've a taste for it, out of perversity or towards some purpose, be that as it may, I was only showing contempt for this bit of cloth, and a bit of cloth doesn't demand you settle accounts. No, I won't bow to you, that is impossible, I'm not that supple, not some freak-show contortionist. That's one of the movements a man can't make, like licking his own arse. I'm not paying for a temptation I haven't felt.

The Dealer   A man can't allow his clothes to be insulted. If the real injustice of the world is the chance of birth, the chance of which place and which hour, the only justice lies in clothes. A man's clothes are, more than the man himself, what he holds most sacred: that about him that does not feel pain; they are the point where justice balances injustice, a point that must not be upset. That's why a man must be judged by his clothes, not by his face, or his arms, or his skin. If it's all right to spit at a man's birth, it's dangerous to spit on the way he rebels.

The Client   Look then, let's come out equal. For a jacket in the dust, I pay with a jacket in the dust. Let's be equals now, equally proud, equally powerless, equally unarmed, equally in pain from cold and from heat. We pay half and half: your semi-nakedness, your half of humiliation, I'm paying for them with half of mine. We still have the other half, still enough to dare meet the other's eye and forget what we've both lost, inadvertently, through risk, through hope, distraction, chance. As for me, I'll still have that anxiety the debtor feels hanging over him even when he has already paid back his debt.

The Dealer   Why do you ask for what you want so abstractly, so intangibly, at this hour of the night, why, when you would have asked for it from somebody else, did you not ask it of me?

The Client   Don't trust the client: he has the air of someone looking for one thing whereas he wants something else, which the seller doesn't suspect, and that he will get in the end.

The Dealer   If you were to flee, I would follow you; if you were to fall under blows from me, I would stay by you till you woke; and if you were to choose not to wake, I'd stay by your side, in your sleep, in your unconscious, and beyond. But I don't want to fight you.

The Client   I'm not afraid of fighting, but I dread rules I'm not familiar with.

The Dealer   There aren't any rules; there are only means; there are only weapons.

The Client   Try to reach out to me, you won't make it; try to wound me: when the blood flows, well then, we'll both bleed, and, inescapably, that blood will unite us, like two Indians by a fire exchanging their blood as savage beasts gather round them. There is no love, there is no love. No, you won't reach anything which isn't already there, because a man dies first, then looks for his death, and meeting it, finally, by chance, on this hazardous journey from one light to another light, he says: So, that's all it was.

The Dealer   Please, amid all the din tonight, did you say anything that you wanted of me and that I wouldn't have heard?

The Client   I've not said anything; I've not said anything. And you, have you, in the night, in this darkness so deep it takes too long to get used to it, have you put anything to me that I might not have discerned?

The Client   Nothing.

The Client   Well then, what weapon?